Florida in the Early 20th Century
Boom and Bust

Katelyn Rice

Consultants

Dorothy Levin, M.S.Ed., MBA
St. Lucie County Schools

Vanessa Ann Gunter, Ph.D.
Department of History
Chapman University

Cassandra Slone
Pinellas County Public Schools

Publishing Credits

Rachelle Cracchiolo, M.S.Ed., *Publisher*
Conni Medina, M.A.Ed., *Managing Editor*
Emily R. Smith, M.A.Ed., *Series Developer*
Diana Kenney, M.A.Ed., NBCT, *Content Director*
Courtney Patterson, *Multimedia Designer*

Image Credits: Cover and pp. 1, 7 (bottom), 8, 17 (left and right), 18–19, 20, 20–21, 24–25, 31 State Archives of Florida; pp. 2–3 R. B. Holt/MPI/Getty Images; p. 4 LOC [LC-DIG-det-4a27966]; p. 5 (right) LOC [LC-USZC4-7551], (left) LOC [LC-USZC4-9027], (top) LOC [sgpwar.19191231]; p. 6 B Christopher/Alamy; p. 7 (top left and right) CSU Archives/Everett Collection; p. 9 Smith Collection/Gado/Getty Images; pp. 10–11 R. B. Holt/MPI/Getty Images; pp. 10, 14 (back and front) Granger, NYC; p. 11 Nigel Cattlin/Science Source; p. 12 FPG/Hulton Archive/Getty Images; p. 13 NARA [12573155]; p. 15 From the Harris & Ewing collection at the Library of Congress; pp. 16–17 State Archives of Florida/Fishbaugh; p. 19 (top) PhotoQuest/Getty Images, (bottom) LOC [LC-DIG-hec-47251]; p. 21 (top) LOC [LC-USZ62-46681]; p. 22 Bundesarchiv, Bild 183-S33882/CC-BY-SA 3.0; p. 23 LOC [LC-USZ62-129812]; pp. 25, 32 Wikimedia Commons/Public Domain; p. 28 LOC [LC-DIG-npcc-00318]; all other images from iStock and/or Shutterstock.

Library of Congress Cataloging-in-Publication Data

Names: Rice, Katelyn, author.
Title: Florida in the early 20th century : boom and bust / Katelyn Rice.
Description: Huntington Beach, CA : Teacher Created Materials, [2017] |
  Includes index. | Audience: 4-6.
Identifiers: LCCN 2016014356 (print) | LCCN 2016016847 (ebook) | ISBN
  9781493835423 (pbk.) | ISBN 9781480756892 (eBook)
Subjects: LCSH: Florida--Economic conditions--20th century--Juvenile
  literature. | Florida--History--20th century--Juvenile literature. |
  Depressions--1929--United States--Juvenile literature.
Classification: LCC F311 .R53 2017 (print) | LCC F311 (ebook) | DDC
  975.9/063--dc23
LC record available at https://lccn.loc.gov/2016014356

Teacher Created Materials

5301 Oceanus Drive
Huntington Beach, CA 92649-1030
http://www.tcmpub.com

ISBN 978-1-4938-3542-3

Table of Contents

A1503

Before the Boom

America went through a lot of growth in the 1800s. But change occurred much more swiftly in the early 20th century. New laws required children to go to school. Women fought for the right to vote. The workforce in the United States was becoming more industrialized.

Men like Henry Ford were making their mark on business. Ford used the **assembly line** to streamline the way cars were built. He was able to build more cars in less time, for less money. This made cars cheaper for the public. More people could buy them.

During the hustle and bustle of this age, there was a state of unrest in Europe. Archduke Franz Ferdinand, heir to the Austro-Hungarian Empire, had been **assassinated**. This led to the start of World War I in 1914. The United States joined the war effort three years later. Millions of U.S. soldiers fought in this war. The war lasted four years. During that time, new technology led to new weapons, such as tanks and aircraft carriers.

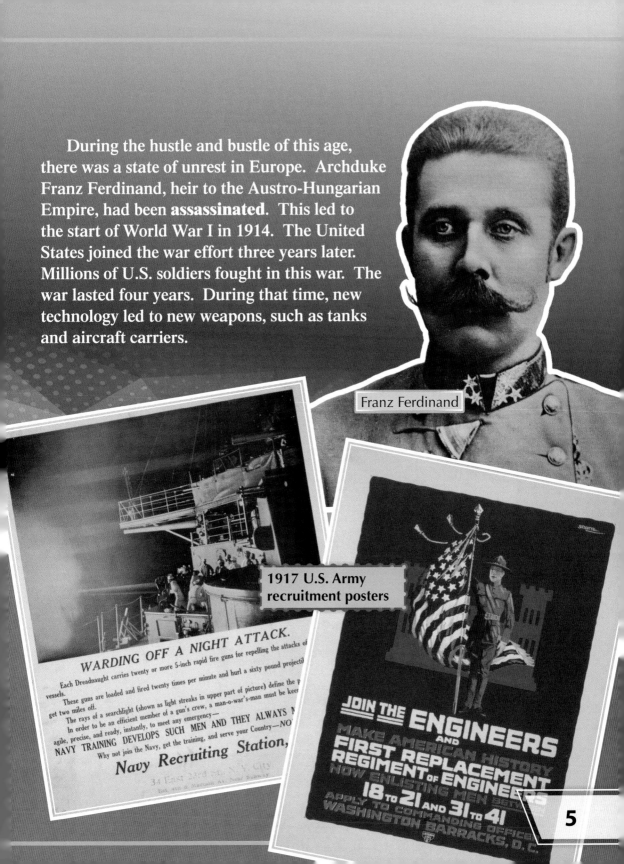

Franz Ferdinand

1917 U.S. Army recruitment posters

WARDING OFF A NIGHT ATTACK.

Each Dreadnaught carries twenty or more 5-inch rapid fire guns for repelling the attacks of vessels.

These guns are loaded and fired twenty times per minute and hurl a sixty pound projectile get two miles off.

The rays of a searchlight (shown as light streaks in upper part of picture) define the p

In order to be an efficient member of a gun's crew, a man-o-war's-man must be keen

agile, precise, and ready, instantly, to meet any emergency—

NAVY TRAINING DEVELOPS SUCH MEN AND THEY ALWAYS

Why not join the Navy, get the training, and serve your Country—NO

Navy Recruiting Station,

34 East 23rd St., N. Y. City

JOIN THE ENGINEERS
AND
MAKE AMERICAN HISTORY
FIRST REPLACEMENT
REGIMENT OF ENGINEERS
NOW ENLISTING MEN BETW
18 TO 21 AND 31 TO 41
APPLY TO COMMANDING OFFICE
WASHINGTON BARRACKS, D.C.

Roaring Twenties

World War I ended in 1918. The years that followed were full of change for the country. Women won the right to vote in 1920. Alcohol was declared illegal to make and sell. Limits were set on the number of immigrants who could move to the country. Jazz and blues music made their way into white culture as many African Americans moved from southern to northern cities.

This period of U.S. history came to be known as the Roaring Twenties. Amid the many cultural changes of the decade, there was an economic boom. People had money to spend. They bought new cars and clothes. Some went to new movie theaters every week. Chain stores, such as Woolworths, popped up all over the country.

By 1930, 12 million U.S. homes had radios. Refrigerators and vacuums made life simpler for many households. But the boom did not last very long. Many people began to buy things on **credit**. They bought more than they could afford to pay for in cash. Little did they know that their spending would come back to haunt them.

1920 advertisement for electric appliances

Mass Culture

Mass culture is a set of ideas that develop when people are influenced by the same media and advertising. Mass culture was prevalent in the 1920s. People liked the same music. They learned the same dance moves. They bought the same clothes.

ABOVE ALL—Your Suit must have Perfect Tailoring. You'll find it here

The CLARA BOW HATS

DESIGNED FOR AND POSED BY THE FAMOUS PARAMOUNT PICTURE STAR

98¢

98¢

Florida's Land Boom

Florida was not exempt from the Roaring Twenties. After World War I, people had time. They had money. Even better, they had automobiles. They were able to travel across the country. Some came to visit Florida. Many were also looking for a new place to live. The area's warm summers and mild winters beckoned many people to the growing state. Almost 300,000 people moved to the state by the early 1920s. Over one million people lived there by the end of the decade.

Most people had to deal with land **speculators**. These people bought land at cheap prices. Then, they sold that land for more than they paid for it. This made the land very costly for others to buy. As a result, people paid some of the money right away. They paid the remainder with credit. They hoped the value of the land would increase, so they could sell it for a profit later.

1922 Miami billboard

Jacksonville, Florida in 1924

Florida Goes Bust

Things in Florida took a turn for the worse around 1926. Money and credit were running out. Fewer people came to the state. Land was just too expensive. The railroads started to shut down. People could not get where they needed to go. Construction supplies could not get to the people who needed them. People who bought land on credit were not able to sell at high enough prices to make their money back. These people lost a lot of money.

This January 1926 magazine cover pokes fun at the Florida land boom.

Mediterranean fruit fly

To make matters worse, two major **hurricanes** hit the state in 1926 and 1928. Streets flooded from all the rain. Homes and shops were destroyed. A massive tidal wave killed many people.

Florida's troubles didn't stop there. Fruit flies plagued the state's **citrus** crops in 1929. Crops were devastated. Citrus production fell by about 60 percent. Farmers struggled to sell enough fruit to pay **taxes** and feed their families. The state's economy was in shambles.

This fruit was damaged by a fruit fly.

This image shows the Miami coastline after the hurricane in October 1926.

Fair, slightly cooler tonight. Friday fair. Fresh southwest to west winds.

89th YEAR—No. 295.

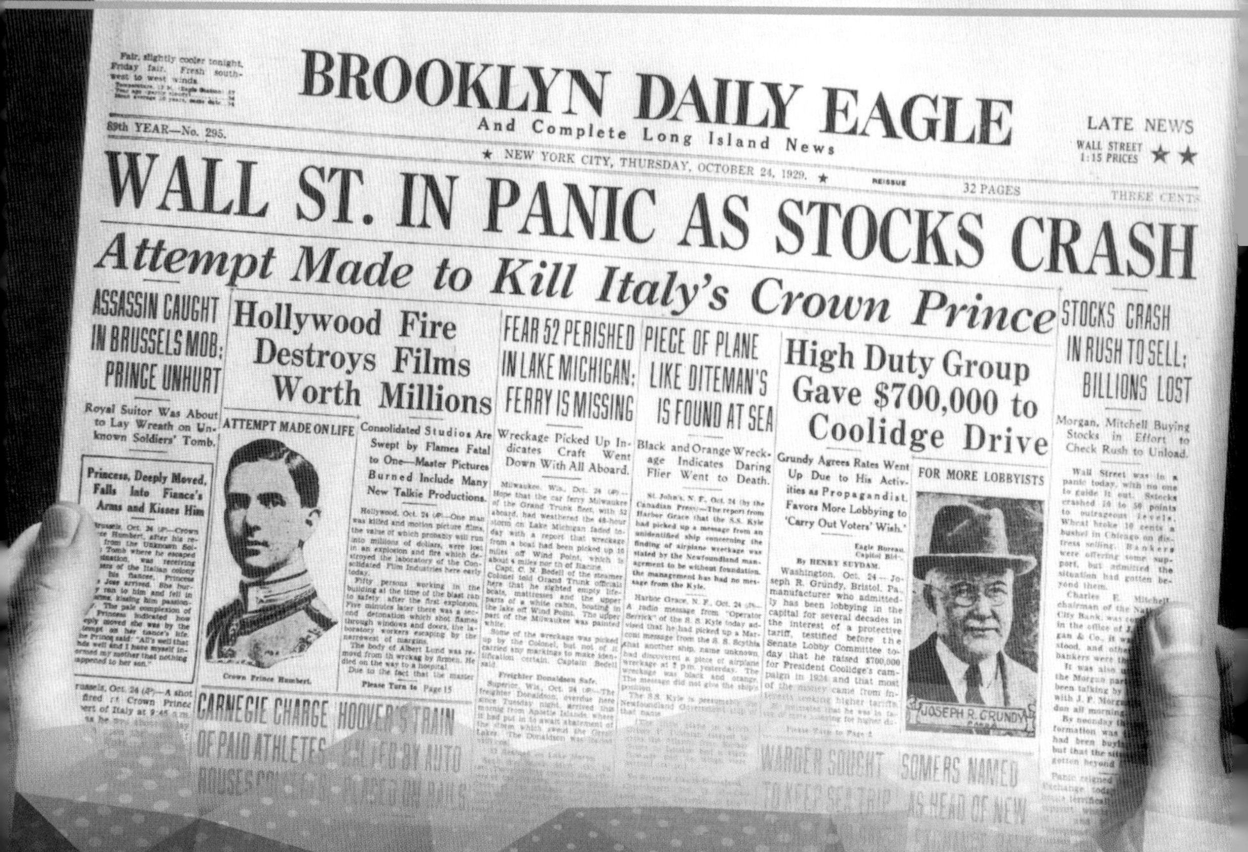

BROOKLYN DAILY EAGLE

And Complete Long Island News

★ NEW YORK CITY, THURSDAY, OCTOBER 24, 1929. ★

32 PAGES

THREE CENTS

LATE NEWS

WALL STREET 1:15 PRICES ★★

WALL ST. IN PANIC AS STOCKS CRASH

Attempt Made to Kill Italy's Crown Prince

ASSASSIN CAUGHT IN BRUSSELS MOB; PRINCE UNHURT

Royal Suitor Was About to Lay Wreath on Unknown Soldiers' Tomb.

Princess, Deeply Moved, Falls Into Fiance's Arms and Kisses Him

ATTEMPT MADE ON LIFE

Crown Prince Humbert.

Hollywood Fire Destroys Films Worth Millions

Consolidated Studios Are Swept by Flames Fatal to One—Master Pictures Burned Include Many New Talkie Productions.

FEAR 52 PERISHED IN LAKE MICHIGAN; FERRY IS MISSING

Wreckage Picked Up Indicates Craft Went Down With All Aboard.

PIECE OF PLANE LIKE DITEMAN'S IS FOUND AT SEA

Black and Orange Wreckage Indicates Daring Flier Went to Death.

High Duty Group Gave $700,000 to Coolidge Drive

Grundy Agrees Rates Went Up Due to His Activities as Propagandist. Favors More Lobbying to 'Carry Out Voters' Wish.'

FOR MORE LOBBYISTS

JOSEPH R. GRUNDY

STOCKS CRASH IN RUSH TO SELL; BILLIONS LOST

Morgan, Mitchell Buying Stocks in Effort to Check Rush to Unload.

CARNEGIE CHARGE OF PAID ATHLETES

HOOVER'S TRAIN

SOMERS NAMED AS HEAD OF NEW

The Nation Goes Bust

The country's economy was not much better than Florida's. On October 29, 1929, the **stock market** crashed. This marked the beginning of the Great Depression. Investors lost $14 billion that day. People panicked. They had bought many things with credit. Many of them had spent more than they could afford. People tried to save the money they had left. They wanted to withdraw their money from the banks. But the banks did not have all the money. They had loaned it to other people.

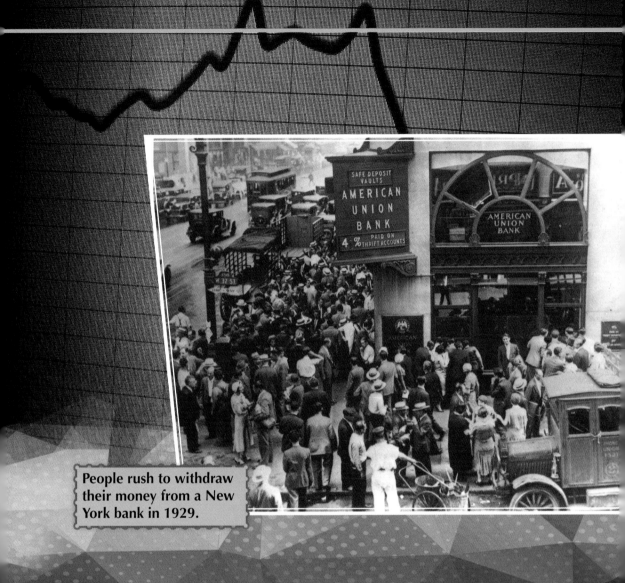

People rush to withdraw their money from a New York bank in 1929.

As a result, people had less money to spend. Businesses sold fewer goods and services. Soon, they had to ask their employees to stay home. They could not afford to pay them their salaries. This made the economy suffer even more.

By 1933, 25 percent of all Americans were unemployed. It was a very dismal time for the nation. Florida had already gone bust. Now, the rest of the country was struggling, too.

FREE
UP COFFEE & DOUGHNUTS
OR THE UNEMPLOYED

FREE SOUP
&

Unemployed men stand in line at a soup kitchen in Chicago.

Many homeless families lived in shanties like this one during the 1930s.

Over 13 million Americans lost their jobs during the Great Depression. People couldn't pay for their homes and land. Some of them turned to crime to take care of their families. They stole food and supplies. They even robbed banks.

But some people had enough to share with others. They started charities that gave people food and clothes. Soup kitchens popped up all over the country. People stood in line for hours just to get a free meal. Many people volunteered to work at soup kitchens. They wanted to help those in need.

A lot of people thought that the government should take care of those without food or homes. Herbert Hoover was the president at the time. He thought people should have to take care of themselves. Many people felt he was doing little to help end the Depression. They blamed him for their troubles. Many people lived in **poverty** until a new president was elected in 1932.

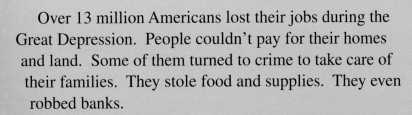

Hoover Flag

Some people blamed President Hoover for the Great Depression. People disliked him so much that they called an empty pocket turned inside out a "Hoover flag."

The Great Depression touched every state. Florida was no different. The state tried to recover, though. In 1931, Florida made gambling on horse and dog races legal. The idea was to tax each bet. This meant that the state would get a small sum of money from each race. But things did not go as planned. Hardly anyone had money to spend!

Crowds gather to watch dog races in Hialeah, Florida.

Hotel owners were hopeful that winter would bring tourists to their businesses. Yet again, there was a problem. The state would not let everyone in. This included tourists. Police waited at the state border. They checked everyone's information. If they didn't have money or a job, they were not allowed into the state—even to visit. The state's government wanted to help people already living there who did not have jobs. It could not afford to help any more people.

1938 map and postcard

Recovery

But all hope was not lost. Change was on the horizon. Franklin D. Roosevelt was elected president in 1932. He started several programs in 1933 that were a part of the **New Deal**. One of those programs was the Civilian Conservation Corps (KOHR). It was formed to give young men jobs. They were given food and clothing, so most of their paychecks could be sent home to their families. Now, more than 40,000 people in Florida were able to work!

People who worked in the programs made Florida a better place. They cut down trees for fire lines. They planted trees. They set up state parks. They even rebuilt the Overseas Railroad. The railroad had been destroyed by a hurricane in 1935. It was important to the state because it connected two pieces of land that were separated by water. Workers got it up and running again by 1938. It helped bring people to Key West.

Civilian Conservation Corps in 1938

Zora Neale Hurston

In the early 1930s, the Federal Writers' Project helped Florida resident Zora Neale Hurston become a well-known author. The Federal Writers' Project was part of the Works Progress Administration. Hurston went on to write more than 50 short stories, essays, and novels.

Fireside Chats

Between 1933 and 1944, President Franklin D. Roosevelt talked to the American people through public radio. During these "fireside chats," he informed listeners about current events and reassured them that everything was going to be okay.

Progress continued in Florida. In 1925, a man named Alfred duPont moved to the state. He was a wealthy man who wanted to help people. He was most concerned for people who lived in the northwest part of the state, also known as the Panhandle. Before the Civil War started in 1861, the Panhandle's economy was booming. But after the war, it was in shambles. DuPont saw it as a place where new businesses could be built. He wanted to start a paper mill in Port St. Joe. He knew it would bring jobs back to the town. Sadly, duPont died in 1935. He never got to see his dreams come true. But the paper mill did open a few years later. It made a lot of money in the years that followed.

A woman works at St. Joe Paper Company in the 1950s.

As the country started to bounce back from the Great Depression, people bought more food. This was good news for Florida's farmers. Now, they could sell more of their crops. More people started to take vacations, too. Some flocked to the beaches. Others visited the hotels around the state. Business in the state was finally picking up.

Hard Work Pays Off

Alfred duPont grew up working in his family's gunpowder business. Later, he started his own company. During that time, he became a multi-millionaire. He even registered over 200 patents for machinery and equipment he invented. One of those was the first gasoline-powered train engine in the United States.

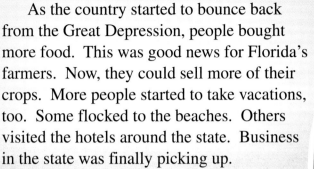

World War II

The dark times were not over yet. Adolf Hitler rose to power in Germany in the early 1930s. In 1938, he announced a plan to merge Germany and Austria. Then, he took over Czechoslovakia (chek-uh-slow-VAW-kee-uh). He wanted to control all of Europe. He planned to attack Poland next. But Great Britain and France didn't want that to happen. They told him that they would declare war if he invaded Poland. In 1939, Hitler used German forces to invade Poland anyway. This started World War II.

Hitler began taking people he deemed "different" from their homes. Race and religion were just two of the reasons Hitler chose to hate people. He sent them to prisons known as **concentration camps**. Under orders from the **Nazi** government, the guards often starved, tortured, and killed people.

Meanwhile, Japan wanted to control Asia and the Pacific. The United States would not trade oil or steel with Japan until it pulled its troops out of China. U.S. troops would not let Japan get oil elsewhere, either. On December 7, 1941, Japan retaliated and bombed Pearl Harbor, a U.S. naval base in Hawaii. The United States entered World War II the next day.

Adolf Hitler

Even though Adolf Hitler was the ruler of Germany, he was not born there. He was actually born in Austria on April 20, 1889.

A Japanese bomber attacks Pearl Harbor.

Over 250,000 U.S. soldiers were from Florida. The state became a hot spot for the military. It was ideal for training. The land was flat. The weather was mild. Many training camps and air stations were built there. Hotels were used to house the rising number of troops in Florida. Some hotels were even turned into hospitals to treat the injured.

People who did not fight in the war helped in other ways. Women, African Americans, and other **marginalized** groups were asked to fill jobs that they were not allowed to have in the past. Some built military cars and planes. Others built tanks. Many women worked in factories while their husbands and sons fought overseas. They worked in shipyards. They worked on farms. The country needed supplies for the war, and Florida was able to provide them. The state's economy flourished.

Protection from the Sun

Benjamin Green was a World War II airman from Miami, Florida. He invented his own sunscreen called Red Veterinary Petrolatum, or Red Vet Pet, in 1944. He used the sunscreen to protect himself and his fellow soldiers from the harmful rays of the sun. This product later became known as Coppertone®.

Soldiers train at Carrabelle Beach in Florida in 1943.

Meanwhile, German **U-boats** were just off the coast. A group of spies from the boats actually made it into the state. In response, the U.S. military set up the Civil Air Patrol. Its job was to prevent more German troops from making it onto U.S. soil. They flew over the water along the state's coast. They reported signs of the enemy. Then, on May 8, 1945, Germany surrendered. Japan quickly followed with its surrender on September 2, 1945. World War II was finally over.

Rosie the Riveter

This picture of Rosie the Riveter was created by Norman Rockwell. She appeared on the cover of the *Saturday Evening Post* in 1943. The fictional character celebrates how women left home to work in factories and support the war effort.

Still Growing

Life was good in the Roaring Twenties. New inventions made life easier for people. Many people were quickly spending money. Many used credit to pay for what they could not afford. This proved to be a risky move.

However, the boom in Florida was short lived. Florida had already gone bust before the country's economy crashed. The stock market crash reminded people that every action has a consequence. The state was slow to recover. But, it eventually did. President Roosevelt helped people find jobs. He helped them rebuild their lives.

World War II brought many more changes to the state. Women and African Americans were asked to take jobs that had typically been reserved for white men. Many others helped with the war effort, too. They helped to reboot the state's economy. The state was on track for growth in the coming decades. More growth was bound to happen. People of the state did not want to let history repeat itself. Today, Florida continues to grow and thrive!

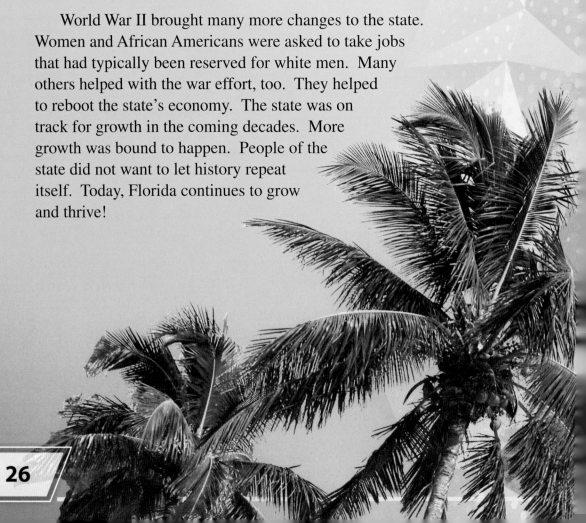

Plan It!

Franklin D. Roosevelt was famous for his fireside chats. These were radio addresses that he gave while he was president. He talked about the issues that people faced in everyday life. Create your own fireside chat about the Great Depression and the programs of the New Deal. Read your chat to a friend or family member.

Franklin D. Roosevelt

Glossary

assassinated—killed for political or religious reasons

assembly line—a line in a factory where a product is built by passing from one station to the next

citrus—a juicy fruit that has a thick skin and grows in warm areas

concentration camps—types of prisons where many people are kept during a war and are usually forced to live in horrible conditions

credit—money a bank or business allows a person to use and then pay back in the future

hurricanes—large, powerful storms that have violent winds

marginalized—a person or group who is kept powerless in society

Nazi—the political party that controlled Germany from 1933 to 1945

New Deal—a program and policy made by Franklin D. Roosevelt to improve conditions during the Great Depression

poverty—the state of having little or no money

speculators—people who invest money in a risky way

stock market—the activity of buying and selling stocks and bonds

taxes—money that people are required to pay a government

U-boats—German submarines

Index

Your Turn!

Women at Work

This picture was created to celebrate how women took jobs to support the war effort. How would you describe this image? What emotions does the picture evoke? Design your own picture to convince people to do something.